The Ultimate G

Welcome!

Thank you for purchasing the Ultimate Guide to Co-Packing. I hope this guide helps you figure out if co-packing is right for your company, how to find the right co-packer, and how to build a better relationship.

Let's jump in!

Navigating the world of co-packing is

- Intimidating
- Confusing
- Frustrating
- Risky
- Rewarding
- Expensive

And more. It's not for the faint of heart. Even though you're having someone else make your product, you're still involved in the management of your business. In other words, the weight of food manufacturing isn't completely off your shoulders.

After reading this guide, you'll have a better idea if you want to take on a co-packer. But first, you've got to answer some tough questions.

Before you head down the co-packing route, there's a couple of things you have to sort out with yourself and your business partners.

Don't brush this step off.

These are the tough questions. The questions no one wants to talk about. The questions you have to work through before you even start your search.

Just like starting up your food business and answering questions like "Where am I going to get the money?" and "Do I want to do this?", getting started with co-packing has it's own set of questions. Lets look at a couple of them:

5 questions to answer before you look for a co-packer:

1. Do I want to give up control of making my product?
Spend some time with this one. It's the most important question, because it fundamentally impacts your business. Do you want to give up control of your manufacturing? For many food producers, they want to be the only one who makes their product. Maybe it comes out better, maybe it's cheaper, or maybe you're a control freak. Ok, I'm kidding about that last one. Regardless, lets look at pros and cons of outsourcing your manufacturing:

Pros:

May be cheaper: Often, outsourcing your manufacturing is cheaper because you don't have the overhead of your own kitchen and you can make a lot more product for the same amount of money,.

More time for sales: Sales drives your food company's growth. So, wouldn't it be great if you had more time to sell your food product? Of course! Outsource your manufacturing and you've got your wish: more time to find new retailers, do store demos, and attend local fairs and festivals.

Less to worry about: Sure, you've got to manage the manufacturing process, but taking the manufacturing off your plate means you have less to worry about. Co-packers worry about equipment breaking, when they're going to schedule you, and the ingredients you have.

Cons

May be expensive: As you'll learn later in the guide, co-packing can be expensive. There are high day rates, storage fees and more that make up the co-packing industry.

Quality control: If you co-pack out of state, quality control is out of your hands. If something goes wrong, your co-packer has to worry about it. You can't do much. This is also true with quality control. Generally, only when you pick up your product do you notice quality issues. That's risky.

Lots of inventory: When someone else is making your product, you've might need to make more product to get your costs down. More product means more cash is tied up in product inventory. And more cash tied up? We all know that may spell doom if you can't seem to move your product fast enough.

It's a tough decision to give up manufacturing your food product, but that's what co-packing is. Let's move on to the next question you need to ask yourself.

2. Do I have the cash to co-pack?

It's no lie - co-packing can quickly empty your bank account. Let's say you have 10 recipes. At upwards of $600-$800 per day, a co-packer is likely to run 2-3 flavors/day. That means 5 days of co-packing. Which really means $3,000 - $4,000. And that's just for your co-packer. Include ingredients and packaging, you're likely to be out $10,000 just for a couple days of manufacturing. See how everything can quickly add up?

Cash is king in any business. And making sure you have enough of it is key to growing your business.

When you're producing in your house, everything is cheap. You have no kitchen rental time to worry about (since you have 24/7 access), you have no employees to pay, and ingredient storage is practically free.

When you switch to co-packing, your company has to pay for all of this - and then some. There are tons of costs associated with co-packing that you don't incur at home. Do you have the cash to make the transition?

Whether the money comes from your current cash reserves, bank loans, credit cards, or friends/family is up to you. Make sure you have some money because if you're going along and all of sudden there's no cash then you have no company. And no company means your products are coming off the shelf.

3. How will you manage everything?
How are you going to oversee quality issues? Who is going to interact with the kitchen manager? Make sure you've got a team member or members to manage everything.

Who is going to make sure you've got enough ingredients? Who is going to make sure you've got recipes and production setup? While many of these responsibilities are part of the co-packers, you're going to want to have a point person to manage everything.

If you're the sole owner of your food biz, you'll manage everything (surprise, surprise). Make sure you've got processes and systems in place (plus **software to run your food business**). You'll be glad to have the system in place before everything goes awry.

4. Is there a co-packer in your area?
Doing an initial co-packer search may yield no results. But, thinking outside your area. Maybe your co-packer is in the next state over. I know many manufacturers who co-pack in Vermont, but they run their companies from all over the place. Kansas, Massachusetts, and New York City for example. But I also know Vermont companies who co-pack out-of-state because there is a co-packer who better meets their company's needs.

Don't like driving 3-5 hours to product your product? Yeah...I don't blame you. Both of my co-packers have never been more than an hour away. But, you may not have any co-packers in your location.

Before you give up because you think there aren't any co-packers in your area, try asking around. Talk with other food producers to see what they do. And who knows - maybe you'll build a shared kitchen (and that's a whole other guide in its own right!).

5. Why do you want to do this?
The final question is more of a personal, introspective question: *Why* do you want to have your products co-packed? A lot of business

owners I've spoken to over the past few years have done it to save tons of time. But, don't just make that your reason.

Think about it. It's important to nail this down. Don't do it because everyone else is doing it.

- Do it because it saves you time
- Do it because it saves you money
- Do it because you get more resources
- Do it because you'll meet industry veterans
- Do it because you want to

And most importantly, do it because it's the right move for your company. After figuring out the outsourcing manufacturing question, this is the second most important question. It can shape your company's future and influence decisions to grow your company.

And remember....

All of these questions should be discussed with anyone who has a major role in your company: business partners, family, friends, business advisors, and even small business consultants (if you use one). You never know when someone is going to suggest something - or connect you with someone - you didn't know beforehand.

Get these questions answered. But them in a word document, write them in your notebook, or just talk about everything face-to-face.

The next section is about why you would even need to consider using a co-packer. And many of the ideas have to do with running your business - not emotionally driven reasons.

Let's move on...

Why would you ever need a co-packer?

You may be wondering why so many food companies co-pack their products. It turns out, there's a lot of business-driven reasons to co-pack.

Why does everything have to be a business decision?

Yes. You make a food product. Yes, you're passionate about it, and yes, it tastes great. But when it comes down to it, you own a light manufacturing company. A company operates around the clock. Problems arise and decisions have to be made.

How you react to problems and opportunities is part of business.

And co-packing is one of those decisions. It's a business decision. Are you going to save money? Are you going to meet demand? You be the judge of that. Here are a couple reasons companies have decided to move from their home or shared kitchen to co-packing:

1. Demand is just too big for your home kitchen

If you can start out in your home kitchen, start there. It's easy to get off the ground. You have low overhead (since you own your house). Plus, consumers are loving the hand-crafted, small-batch movement. Only when you make something in your house can you call it "homemade".

But sometimes, **consumer demand goes beyond your stovetop** and out of your single oven.

First of all, congrats! It's a big move to get out of the house. I've done it with one of three companies. It's scary, fun, exhilarating, and absolutely terrifying at the same time. Plus, growing a food business is tough when you're competing with over 120,000 other products in the grocery store. This is a huge milestone. Congratulations!

Ok, let's get serious...

What does that mean for your little food biz?

You need to produce in larger quantities. And that means leaving the kitchen you've called home for the past year or two. That means you've got to look at other options in your area. One of those options is co-packing. As you work through this guide you'll learn if co-packing is the right decision for you.

2. You need to abide by state laws

Not everyone has the luxury of starting their food business from their home kitchen. Only 14 states have the right to pre-heat their stoves. And even then, they may only be able to produce baked goods - not a process food like mustard, BBQ sauce, or marinades. Consider yourself lucky.

What laws are there to abide by?

- FDA-inspected facility
- Food Safety Modernization Act
- USDA Laws & Regulations (only if you handle raw meat products)
- Third-Party Audit Certification (needed if you want to sell to Whole Foods)

And that's just a short list. These laws force people to manufacture outside their home. It dramatically increases start-up costs, but it's the same reason many states lack small-batch goodies - it's simply too expensive to start. I know, it's unfortunate many Americans haven't experienced the creativity of small food companies.

If you're in a state where home bakeries and processing isn't permitted, look into leasing commercial kitchen space to get started. You should only look at co-packing when you have the demand to sustain it (see #1).

3. You'd rather sell your product

Let's face it. Being stuck in a kitchen leaning over a 190 degree kettle isn't glamorous. You smell like your product, machines break, and you never get around to doing anything else. That means limited selling, networking, and business development.
If you have limited time to sell, you have limited time to build your business.

It's a harsh reality of the food industry. Many small food producers are stuck making their product and don't have time to sell it and build a business. Sure, you could outsource the sales function, but nobody sells your product better than you do.

That's why co-packing is a smart move.

Co-packing gives you the flexibility to be the sales person you want to be. Want to build a hot sauce empire? You've got the time now. Want to be represented by distributors across the country? You've got the time.

Remember, the only way you'll stay in business is if you can move enough cases of your products to be profitable. And to do that, you may need to let other people manage certain parts of your business.

Plus, moving more product means you're growing your business. And that means you can quit that pesky full-time job of yours. Oh, and speaking of jobs...

4. You work full-time and need someone else to make the product

Working 50-60 hours a week on top of slaving over a stove to make jam is not an ideal work-life balance. Things can get crazy pretty fast - long nights, equipment breaking, you know the deal.

Many of you need to have another income to support your dream of running a food business.

Just like you, I worked full-time while growing my company. Yes, it inhibited growth for a few years, but I needed to support myself. As I grew my company, the after-work hours weren't enough to meet demand.

I needed a change.

That's when I turned to co-packing. If I could have someone else make my product with my oversight, I could devote my after-work and weekends hours to building a business. You can do the same thing!

If you're exhausted from working full-time, plus running a part-time food business, think about co-packing. Trust me, the first run will totally be worth it.

Think about it: no more chopping produce, no more smelling like your product for days, and my personal favorite -- no more capping. That's what you pay someone else to do. Assuming you have the money to pay for a co-packer (which is more likely if you have a full-time job), it's worth it's weight in gold to build your dream while someone else manufacturers your product.

Once you establish a relationship with your co-packer, and you're ready to leave your full-time job, you'll have TONS of time for sales, meeting with new retailers, doing store demos, etc. This is the ideal situation. That is, of course, if you like sales and marketing! If you don't, keep making your product and hire an outside sales team. But, that's a whole other book in its own right!

5. You can't find your own kitchen space.

Finding kitchen space is flat-out hard. No one has to tell you that. Some companies search for kitchen space for years. Whether you're looking for the perfect co-packer, a shared kitchen to help you grow, or a restaurant kitchen to rent, you may never find kitchen space.

And not to mention the possibility of your own kitchen space - that's just plain expensive, time consuming, and from other producers I've talked to, quite the nightmare.

What this comes down to is you need a place to make your product.

You can't go too long without producing, right?. This means you need to find a kitchen to quickly meet demand. That really means co-packing is one of the best solutions. Here's a couple reasons why:

1. If you have recipes ready, co-packers can ramp up quickly

2. You can often produce what you need, when you need it
3. It may, financially, be a better move for your company (no multi-year lease to deal with)
4. Buying equipment to better fit your co-packer is better than buying the *whole* kitchen.
5. (I'll reiterate this one) You have time for sales!

Kitchen searching requires you to be flexible.

If you're looking for a kitchen and things aren't panning out, look at your requirements. Maybe you don't need that much storage space. Maybe you don't need an enormous bottling line.

You may have to sacrifice a few things to find the perfect kitchen. But always keep a co-packer in mind when something's just not working for you.

What it comes down to is this:

You need to find the manufacturing solution that works best for you and your company. If that's producing by yourself, keep doing that. If that's choosing to have someone else produce for you that works, too. Take time to weigh your options. Talk to friends, family, other food producers, business advisors, etc. Get everyone's opinion. But remember, it's ultimately your decision.

The rest of this ebook assumes you've taken the plunge to search for and work with a co-packer to produce your product. Even if you'd still like to produce in your own kitchen, I urge you to read the rest of the guide. It may shed light on some problems you've been having in your own production or spark ideas to adapt for your own business.

Let's press on!

So you've made the decision to get your product co-packed.

Pop open a bottle of champagne - that's awesome! Seriously, though - it's a big decision. Congrats! It also means your company is growing. Typically, companies choose co-packing when demand for their product increases to a point they can't handle it anymore.

Let's get right to it then, shall we?

There's a lot to know about co-packing your product. It's nothing short of a complicated process. There are many moving parts. To break it down, I wrote this guide in sections.

Here's just a few things you'll learn:

- How to find a co-packer in your area
- Selecting the right co-packer for you
- How much it costs to work with a co-packer (plus hidden cost they don't tell you about)
- The top three secrets to a good co-packing relationship
- How to have the co-packer go beyond just making your product
- What happens if you need to switch co-packers?

It's a *ton* of information. And it's organized as best as possible to make it not only easy for you to digest, but you'll even learn something, too. Wherever possible, there are actionable steps for you to build out your co-packing plan so that you're not meeting with co-packers without knowing anything (plus, that's super embarrassing).

How the guide is structured:

- Summaries - Cliff notes just for you
- Lists and bullets - Easy, quick, digestible points so you don't have to read every word.
- Real-life stories - Where possible, I include my personal stories from working with several co-packers.
- Worksheets - In the appendix, there are worksheets to help you make the best decision possible when it comes to selecting and working with a co-packer.
- Frequently Asked Questions - A quick Q&A of questions I've been asked over the years.

Now that I've covered the structure of the guide, it's time to get to the meat of this guide: how to select and work with a co-packer to bring your company's products to the next level. First up is the question I get most often:

How do I find a co-packer? Let's explore your options.

How to Find a Co-Packer

This is the step that takes the longest amount of time. You can't work with just any co-packer. They have to have the right equipment, be priced right, and you have actually like the people who make your product. Sounds stupid, but believe me, being friends with your co-packer pays in spades when you're in a jam.

The search to find the perfect co-packer is a long, detailed process. It's near impossible to even *know* the companies that co-pack in your area. Sure, you could do a quick Google search, but often times co-packing companies are hiding in the weeds (plus, they're not exactly pros at search engine optimization).

That's why I've got a few ideas to help you find your co-packer.

Three Ways to Find a Co-Packer in Your Area:

As I said above, finding a co-packer isn't as simple as a Google search. The two co-packers I've used have both been found by word of mouth. Yes - it still works! Here are a couple avenues you can take to start making a list.

1. Ask other food producers

This is how I found my co-packers. I simply struck up a conversation with other food producers, either at events or farmer's markets. It's not like it's a secret or anything. Food producers will tell you where their product is made. After all, it gets them in good graces with their kitchen manager.

But, there's a right way to approach this. Don't just walk up to a producer and ask "Where is your product made?" -- that's like walking up to a girl in the bar and kissing her before saying hello (Ok, maybe not, but you get the idea).

Engage in conversation. Ask them about their process, when they started, their favorite flavor, what they've learned in the industry. Get to know them for a little bit. Then, when you feel you have a certain level of trust, ask about referrals (not only about co-packing, but ingredient suppliers, packaging suppliers, etc).

This helps the other producer feel comfortable. Plus, they may actually produce in their own kitchen. And, they may not have considered co-packing for other people as another revenue source. It's not ideal because it takes away from their time to market their company, but it could be an avenue to larger equipment to meet demand and then phase over to co-packing product.

If they do use a co-packer, you're in luck!

Many food producers speak highly of their co-packer and happy to refer you. Why would they do that? They might get a referral bonus! With my second co-packer, the hot sauce vendor who referred me got a couple free cleanings (Yep - he makes the kitchen quite messy).

How to make the co-pack referral work for you:

1. Ask for their company information (or just take a business card)
2. Ask for the co-packers information
3. Get a general idea of how they operate. That way, you already have questions.
4. Follow up that day or the following day - post three sticky notes if you have to - Don't forget!
5. Follow up again if you don't hear back within 3-5 business days. (Yes, seriously)

Further in the guide, you'll learn how to handle the first co-packer meeting and what questions to ask. For now, we're still trying to find you a co-packer. Let's make that job one (or, if you want to, speed ahead to the section about visiting co-packers for the first time).

Let's explore the next way to find a co-packer: industry websites.

2. Look on food industry websites

There are numerous industry websites to find a co-packer (and learn a TON about running and growing your food business). Here are 10 links to industry sites with multiple conversations on finding a co-packer. The first few are LinkedIn groups. The rest are indpendent sites.

1. **FoodBiz Startup**
2. **Gourmet Professionals Who Sell Online**
3. **Food Marketing Group**
4. **Cornell School of Food Science**
5. SpecialtyFood.org has a **list of co-packers** throughout every state (not a full list, though)
6. **SmallFoodBiz.com**
7. **Foodpreneur.com**
8. **Nebraska Food Processing Institute**
9. **NC State University Food Science Extension**
10. **FindaCoPacker.com** (an infrequently updated directory)

These may not be in your location, but many of these sites have forums you can post on to find a co-packer closer to you. Regardless, bookmark these sites so you can refer back to them. They provide a great avenue for you to meet other food producers and ask questions about starting, running, and growing your business.

3. Contact your state agriculture department

You'll notice a couple of those links above are links to state agriculture departments that have specific food processing programs. These are goldmines of information. The team of employees at the state level know almost everything there is to know about food business -- including finding a co-packer. They'll be glad to help you out.

Here are a few links to the most popular state agriculture departments:

Vermont
New York
California
Nebraska
New Hampshire
Massachussetts

Ask for the person who works with small food producers. They'll know exactly what you're going through and give you the resources to build your food business - not just help you find a co-packer.

What if you can't find your department of agriculture or they're low on available resources?

Your next best bet is to work with the small business administration.

There are local chapters all over the place, plus the counseling is 100% free. Here's a list of **all the small business development centers in the nation**. Get in touch with your local chapter. They'll get you set up with an advisor.

Why work with an SBDC advisor?

They know the landscape. They've likely worked with other food producers facing the same problems, and they have a network that extends far beyond just family and friends. If they don't know where you can find a co-packer, chances are they have a client who can.

Bottom line: take advantage of state agencies. It's free - like zero dollars. They offer tons of resources, free advice, and someone to talk things through with.

As you navigate the crazy world of co-packing, it's nice to have someone to listen to your challenges and help you make a decision. Plus, the SBDC folks are good with numbers, so they'll make sure you're making money, too. Always a plus.

After all of this talking with state agencies and figuring out where other food producers make their product, you may not end up with a co-packer to make your product.

What happens if you can't find a co-packing space?

Take a deep breathe. Maybe you found a co-packer but their not ready for you or don't have the space in their production schedule. This is often the case with co-packers who have anchor tenants (large food producers who pay to keep the space open - rent, lights, etc. But, that's because they're there a lot producing their products. They are supported by a bunch of small producers (like you) who take up the remaining time the kitchen sits idle.

Whatever the reason is, **if you don't find a co-packer, it's not the end of the world.** There simply might not be space in your area. It's entirely possible co-packers are at their max in regards to the number of products they can produce. And getting a bigger facility doesn't exactly happen overnight.

So, where does that leave you?

You could start your own co-packing kitchen, but then you'd be a co-packer -- not a food producer. My current co-packer is balancing time between making other products (like mine) and finding the time to keep shelves stocked with her own product line, too. It's a delicate balance I'm sure you don't want to get into.

Opening your own facility is off the table. What's next?

Turns out you might have to get creative. There are tons of options to make large batches of product to meet demand. While not the subject of this guide, lets quickly look at a couple of them:

1. Church kitchen
Depending on what you're producing, church kitchens are a great place to make larger quantities of product. There won't be a filler or labeling machine, but you get access to a state-certified commercial kitchen.

2. High school (or any school) cafeteria

I've been in my fair share of school cafeterias and they rival any other kitchen establishment I've seen. Just like churches, the equipment is limited. Plus, you may not be able to produce certain products because of allergies. But, you may be able to get in here for free. It's worth a shot.

3. Restaurant (after hours)

I know several food producers who produce after local restaurants have closed their doors. It's called the graveyard shift. While it's obviously not ideal, some food producers love to make their product so much that they'll make it in the wee hours of the morning before the restaurant opens for breakfast. Have you thought about asking a local restaurant to use their kitchen? Nothing ventured, nothing gained.

4.Shared Kitchen

Is there a shared kitchen in your area where multiple producers share the space? There are several here in Vermont and throughout the northeast. They may be a great stepping stone for your business while you reach a certain volume with your product. See the tips above regarding asking producers about a co-packer to find a shared kitchen in your town (or at least close by.)

Selecting the Right Co-Packer for Your Food Business

If you're lucky, you've got several co-packers to choose from. If not, you'll have to make your co-packer work until you can find another facility or open your own. If you have the luxury of choosing, read on.

Finding the best co-packer for the job is tough.

There's so many factors at play: space, time, money, capabilities, current kitchen tenants etc. Everything should influence your decision. Why? Because when and if you have to switch co-packers, it costs a lot of money and time to move everything over.

This section helps you make the right decision the first time.

Below, you'll find a list of things to consider as you tour different kitchens, meet kitchen managers, talk with current producers, and assess the company. This is by no means an exhaustive list, but gives you a great starting point.

12 Things to Consider When Selecting a Co-Packer

1. Size of the facility
How big is the kitchen? Is there enough room for you to produce? And don't forget: take into account any space you'll need should you have to bring in a specific piece of equipment to produce your product. I've produced in 700 square foot kitchens and 7,000 square foot kitchens. Both have met my needs, but the smaller space has met my needs better.

Think storage space, too.

You've got to keep everything stored there (or truck it in and out for each production). And by everything, I mean raw materials/ingredients, all of your packaging (glass jars, plastic caps, labels, boxes, hang tags, etc), and if you ship out of the facility, your finished goods will also need a pallet to stay on.

You're not the only producer.

There may be a number of producers who already lay claim to much of the space. The question you (and the production manager) have to answer is, "is there enough room for your company to move in?" Large kitchens (3,000 square feet and up) tend to have space for a certain number of manufacturers. If you don't get a meeting with a co-packer, it could be because they're at capacity in their facility.

2. Number of employees
A typical co-packer is made up of 3-5 employees. I explain who below, but bring it up as a concern because you may need more than one person to help co-pack for you. In my experience, it's taken a team of 3 people to make 80 gallons of mustard - sometimes 4 or 5 if the facility is under a time crunch.

Does the kitchen you're looking at have enough employees?

It's something to consider. Are you going to hop in and help if something goes wrong? I've helped on several productions because it's my company on the line. We needed product to meet large purchase orders. As a small producer, you hope for enough team members, but sometimes it doesn't happen.

Ask about part-time help.

Does the co-packer you're looking at bring in help when they need it or are you responsible for finding extra help. One co-packer I know has an army of part-time workers who are called on when she needs help the most. All of them are great people willing to lend a hand. Truth is, the kitchen manager isn't going to always be the only one handling your product. That means you should meet as many people as possible when you go for a tour.

Now, on to who typically makes up a co-packer's staff:

General Manager
This is the person who runs the show. They were likely instrumental in getting funding to open the facility. They know if you'll fit in the schedule. And they have a general outlook on the industry.

Kitchen Manager
Sometimes the same person as the General Manager. The Kitchen Manager is the one who oversees and participates in all of the productions, 5 days a week. They know how to make every product, how much product they can make in an 8-hour day, and if you'll be able to produce your product on the equipment currently in the kitchen. It's also likely this person is ServSafe certified (mandatory for third-party certified kitchens -- more on that later in the list).

Food Scientist
These guys are the brains behind the operation. They know everything there is to know about food processing - from pH to fill temperature, acidified foods, to scaling recipes. They're knowledge

is indispensable. Make sure someone knows something about food science at the co-packing facility.

1-2 production assistants
Need help weighing out ingredients, filling or labeling product? These people handle all the nitty gritty at the facility - even washing the dishes. As mentioned above, there may be more than 2 of these people because they rotate in and out.

Small Business Advisors (optional)
One of the leading shared kitchen & co-packing incubators in Vermont has a small business development liason's office in the building. This is super helpful to producers because now they have business planning and consulting (free, I might add) at their disposal. While this is likely to not be a position in many co-packing facilities, business management cannot be overlooked.

3. Production capability
How many units can the facility pump out in a day? Would they have to produce every day to meet your demand? If they do, it's not a good fit. But, make sure they can produce on a regular schedule. The last you want is to be stuck with no product and purchase orders out your ears with no available kitchen time.

Plus, look at what equipment they have.

Do you need to furnish any special equipment to produce your product? Or, does the kitchen have everything you could ever dream of? Make sure to ask specific questions about equipment. And if they don't something you need, see if you need to buy it outright or if the facility would be willing to purchase one for you if you sign a year-long contract. (More on that in the pricing section later).

Production capacity is important because you may be growing, too. What starts out as 50 cases of product a month may double or triple (like it did for me). That means you need to find a facility that can grow with you - not just one for your current needs. Keep that in mind.

4. Distance from your home

Pretty sure you don't want to drive hours to your co-packing space. That would be crazy on so many fronts.

That means, you need to take proximity into account.

Find a kitchen that's close by. Otherwise you'll feel like all you do is drive back and forth - wasting both time and money. Two resources that are limited, right?

On a personal note, **we used to drive an hour each way to our first co-packer.** I chose to drop or ship all of my ingredients (to avoid a fee you'll learn more about later). Sometimes, that meant driving back and forth 2-3 days a week. That ate up a lot of time I could have used to sell more product.

Currently, we're 15 minutes from our co-packer. It's made all the difference. I can coordinate more local deliveries of perishable product, if there's an emergency, it's easier for me to fix it, and well, the most obvious advantage being that my product is closer to me if I need it.

For some of you, you may have to drive long distances. On the plus side, the gas can be written off as a business expense, but don't you want to be able to have time to build your company? Then travel distance should be taken into account when selecting a co-packer.

5. Receiving capability
Your ingredients, labels, and packaging have to make it to the kitchen, right? Figuring out how that happens is important when you're selecting a co-packer. Here's a couple receiving tips/questions to keep in mind:

Is someone always there?
Not only do you frustrate the UPS delivery man when no one is at your co-packer, but it's frustrating for you, too. Make sure you know when and where to have deliveries dropped off. Why so important? Think about this: if you have refrigerated or frozen product being delivered, it has to stay at a certain temperature. Your butter or eggs can't be left outside in the summer - that would just cost you a ton of money.

Do they have a forklift?
This is going to be kitchen dependent. If the kitchen is less than 3,000 sq ft, it's likely there's no room for a forklift. But, if you're getting a pallet of all-purpose flour delivered, you probably don't want to move it bag by bag. That's why a forklift comes in handy. You can transport product from one end of the kitchen to the other.

Is there a loading dock?
Chances are you're going to have to bring in a lot more raw materials than at your previous kitchen. That makes a loading dock handy. Large semi-trucks can pull up to the receiving area and simply slide a pallet off their truck. Without a loading dock, you have to request a liftgate from the trucking company and there's an extra fee for the liftgate. But, it makes your new co-packer super happy when they don't have to climb onto the truck to disassemble a pallet with over 300 cases of glass jars (Yep - I've been there!). Bottom line: Get a liftgate on the delivery truck or ask if there's a loading dock at your co-packing kitchen.

How do deliveries work?
Many co-packers are logistical nightmares. There's deliveries coming in daily, product being made daily, and employees needed to handle large drop-offs. That's why it's smart to learn how deliveries work at the co-packer. Can they only come on certain days? Are there weight restrictions? And what about deliveries that take up all of your storage space?

It's best to iron out these details before you sign anything. That way you know exactly what you're getting into. For example, at my current co-packer it requires a little more leg work, but I don't pay a premium for it because I'm doing the extra work - even with deliveries. It's important though - you'll be sending materials to the kitchen all the time. It's best to know how it works.

6. Pricing structure
This is its own section later in the guide, but I'll give you the quick version now. Co-packing pricing can be some of the most confusing pricing you'll ever see. It's not as simple as a $99 one-time fee or buy-one-get-one-free. It gets much crazier.

How co-packers price their service

There are two main ways co-packers price. The first way is a flat day-rate. It could be anywhere from a couple hundred bucks all the way up to $1,000 or more. This is the way I started out at my first co-packer. I paid a day-rate. That forced me to crank out as many units as I could on each day. Why? Because the more units I produced, the lower my labor rate was. It's the only cost factor I could leverage.

The other way to charge is a per unit price. This is often figured out after you and co-packer meet to go over how your product is produced, how many people it takes, is there downtime, do things sit overnight, etc. Based on time involved (including prep), your unit price may fluctuate as I'll discuss later. Per unit pricing is nice because you can predict your unit costs more accurately.

Where many co-packers get you

There are all sorts of fees when you start to work with co-packers. Everything from receiving fees to consulting and storage. Again, these are listed out later in the guide.

Work through your numbers early

Whatever pricing gets handed to you when you engage with a co-packer, make sure you work through the numbers to see if you're still going to make money. You do want to make money, right? If you're going to be producing a guaranteed amount, you may want to look into contracting so that you get a flat rate throughout the year. It's not only about the price of your product when it leaves the warehouse, but it also means your profit margins throughout the distribution channel.

7. Owner & employee personality

If I had to highlight an item on this list with stars and big giant arrows, it's this one. You have got to get along with your co-packer. They're basically married to you. You spend time with them, you have hard conversations, and you are in constant communication. You've got to be nice to them, just like they have to be nice to you -- or things get rocky.

And, I know -- sometimes, you won't know someone's true colors until a few months (or maybe years) down the road. It's hard to gauge someone's personality from an hour-long meeting. That's why you should make sure you could work with this person.

Let me tell you a quick story:

My first co-packer started out as a great relationship. She was nice, attentive, and got the job done (albeit at a pricey rate). But, months in, my phone calls weren't being returned, errors were being made in production (costing me more money), and I felt pushed aside for larger contracts they were dealing with.

Lesson learned? Make sure you'd jump in front of a bus for your co-packer. They have your baby, your recipes, in their hands. Make sure it's someone you mesh with, you trust and you can openly communicate with. Funny, sounds a little bit like marriage, doesn't it?

8. Shipping capability

Producing a lot of product means you're moving a lot of product, too. And that means your co-packer has to keep up with what's being shipped where. Some co-packers take care of your finished product leaving the kitchen - other's don't. Why is this important?

You may need a pallet moved, an online order packed up, or a couple cases shipped off to a regional retailer. Find out if your co-packer does this. If they do, it's likely going to cost you - either per shipment, case, or unit. The alternative, however, is you picking up all the product and shipping it yourself - tons of time - so figure out if it's worth it or not for you.

What do I do?

I pick up all of my manufactured product and store it in my basement. I use my co-packer as a pick-up location for distributors. I take care of direct orders, online shipments, and events and festivals. Plus, I know how much of each variety I have on-hand.

9. Third-party certifications (and health inspections)

The last thing you want to do is produce your product in a kitchen that isn't up to code - or worse - it's just plain dirty. Check for cleanliness and other health records showing your potential facility has been cleaned. And while you're at it, check for other certifications.

There are tons of health and allergen-related permits and certifications. From gluten-free to kosher and organic, the list is endless. And you want to find out if your co-packer is certified.

But, be careful. Some facilities may call themselves gluten-free and not be certified. That means you can't put gluten free on your label. It has to be from a certified facility. But, more on that later - we're getting off topic.

These certifications make it so that many companies are able to lay claim to the many "free statements." But the certifications don't end there.

Your facility also has to abide by state and FDA guidelines. For example, in Vermont, the department of health requires every manufacturer (not just the kitchen) be certified. That means the local health inspector needs to see your production process and make sure the facility is in tip-top shape. And your co-packer is going to have you fit the bill because it's a lot of time and money to get ready for inspections. Time your co-packer could be using to make someone else's product.

Another reason you want to check up on third-party audits and certifications is it may depend on your company's growth. Whole Foods, one of the major grocery store chains requires your product be produced in a third-party certified kitchen. No certification? No Whole Foods.

Make sure the kitchen has proof of certification before you move forward - yes, it's that important!

10. Other customer experiences

Let's say you just moved to town and you're looking for the best pizza around. What would you do? Check online? Find Yelp reviews? Or, would you ask your trusting friends and family?

The testimonial and experience of others probably heavily influences your decision of where to grab the best pizza ever. Because your friends know the good hangouts and the places to avoid.

The same is true with co-packers. You'll learn a lot about the kitchen from the companies that already produce their products there. But, how do you find out who produces there? Just ask.

See if your co-packer will give you contact information to other manufacturers. Ask how long they've been producing there and see if you could get in touch with them. And what should you ask them? Here are a couple questions to ask:

1. Have you had any challenges with co-packing?
Food producers are honest people. They'll tell you if it's been challenging co-packing. Sure, it may change your opinion or co-packaing, but what better way to find out about co-packing than asking people who already do it?

2. What's it like working with the kitchen manager?
Again, honesty here is great, too. Kitchen managers are typically one or the other - good or bad. Other producers will let you know which one their manager is. And hopefully it's good. Keep in mind, the kitchen manager may only give you success stories - not other producers who may give you the honest truth. Get to know them through other people and then make your own decision.

3. Would you change anything about the facility?
No co-packer is perfect - there's flaws in every facility. Talk to other producers to find out what your potential co-packer's weaknesses are. Maybe it's hard to make deliveries or schedule a production. Producers will tell you what's wrong the facility (and what they'll do the

4. Are you able to produce to demand?

You want to know if there are any production bottlenecks, right? And what about producing to meet a spike in sales? What if you have a huge press hit and product is flying out the door? You want to know if your co-packer will be able to meet the demand. Other customers will have a good gauge for this based on their own experiences.

11. Equipment needs

You can expect the majority of co-packers to have the same standard equipment. From a six-burner stove to a kettle, kitchen wares to a three-bay sink, there are certain pieces of equipment a commercial kitchen needs. But, lets explore the equipment that would make your co-packing experience easier (and cheaper).

Here's a list of the "nice-to-haves" in a co-packing kitchen:

Large kettles

You're not going to be able to produce the product you need with a stock pot - or even a 5 gallon tabletop kettle. Co-packers should have at least one 40-gallon kettle (or two 20 gallon kettles like my current co-packer). This allows you to make enough product and justify the additional cost of co-packing. After all, you should be moving some serious product if you're considering co-packing.

Commercial Immersion Blender

Definitely kettle's best friend right here. Stop mixing ingredients with a paddle (those are necessary, too) and pick up a **commercial immersion blender from Waring**. But, be careful, this thing blends like no other. Oh, and if you don't want everything coming together (meaning, you still need chunks of something like tomatoes), stick with the good old fashioned paddle. Sidenote: another added benefit of commercial blenders? Awesome biceps. It's pretty heavy so you might want to hit the gym for some arm curls. Ok, I kid, I kid.

Automatic (or pedal-powered) Filler - dry and wet

I think filling machines are cooler than any home kitchen appliance. They save an incredible amount of time and keep your product's net fill weight as close to what's on the label as possible. Gone are the days of hand filling your product. If co-packers don't have an automatic filler, check for a pedal-powered one. All that means is the filler is activated by stepping on a pedal with your foot to fill each jar. This is more likely at smaller co-packers.

Labeling machine (there are tons out there)

I have a confession to make: Our products are still hand-labeled. Yes, my co-packer is tiny and they haven't invested in a labeling machine. And yes, that means your co-packer should have one. Hand-labeling takes forever and sometimes the labels don't go on straight. While labeling machines aren't perfect either, they certainly help to speed things up. And when you're producing over 1,000 units a day, believe me, you want as much automation as possible. Viva la labeler!

Horizontal and/or Vertical Band Sealer

It was like Christmas when this arrived at my house a few years ago. We purchased a horizontal band sealer off eBay for my energy bar company. It helped us package 500 bars a day from our home kitchen. Sure, it broke a few times and requires some black electrical tape, but the seal was great, the small conveyor belt sped things up, and we were cranking. Make sure your co-packer has one of these if you're manufacturing any bagged items that need to be sealed like nuts, granola, cereals, or dry mixes. It will save your life. Guaranteed.

There's tons more equipment that should make it on to the "nice-to-haves" list, but we've got to move on to answering another question:

What if your co-packer doesn't have the equipment you need?

While I hope this doesn't happen to you, you may find co-packers in your area don't have the equipment you need. Don't panic. It happens all the time. They simply haven't produced a product like yours. Here are three options to remedy the situation:

1. Have the co-packer purchase the equipment

While unlikely, you might be able to get your co-packer to purchase the equipment for you. Why? Because it likely benefits them. They're able to bring in more producers because they have the equipment. Plus, it'll help get your product produced faster. Keep in mind the co-packer will likely want to have you sign a year-long contract before they purchase equipment for you. That way, they know they'll have a consistent revenue stream from you and be able to justify the added expense.

2. Split the cost with your co-packer

I've done this one and it's worked out great. When we switched co-packers, the new place didn't have a commercial immersion blender (see above about why it's so awesome). I explained the benefits to the kitchen manager and we agreed to split it. Now, it's used by almost every producer and is a great addition to the kitchen's equipment line up. This is the best way to go if you don't have the funds to buy the equipment outright.

3. Finance the equipment yourself

And probably the most popular way to get new equipment in the door, financing equipment yourself is likely to happen at some point. Co-packers don't want to take the risk on you, they might not have the room, and just like you, they may not have the cash flow to split the purchase. Here are a couple tips if you're looking to finance equipment yourself:

- Shop around - look for used equipment at auctions or restaurant equipment stores.
- Test the equipment - especially used. You want to know it works before you bring it in.
- Loan options - from crowd-funding to bank loans, and credit cards, explore your options.

I'm no banker, but if you can finance a piece of equipment to make your life easier (for you and your co-packer), I'd do it. Worst case scenario is you re-sell the equipment if it isn't right for you.

Remember, you don't have to cut ties with your co-packer if they don't have the equipment you need. Make it work by using some of the strategies above. On to the final point.

12. Scheduling production

Wouldn't it be horrible if you had outstanding purchase orders you couldn't fill? It'd be even worse if you couldn't get kitchen time to meet demand, wouldn't it? Obviously, you can't plan for every spike in demand, but it's something to consider when selecting your co-packer. Here are a few questions to ask when you meet with your co-packer:

- How many units of my product can you produce in a day?
- How many days in advance should I schedule my productions?
- What happens if I need to change or cancel a production?
- Is there a community calendar to see when there is kitchen time available?

Again, while it's not an exhaustive list, it's important to know how co-packers run their kitchens. The last thing you want to have happen is have no kitchen time in the middle of your busy season. That means plan ahead.

Tip: Look at your previous year's sales. Forecast an increase and schedule more productions when you're at your peak.

Just like buying a house, the requirements list to select a co-packer is daunting (and to think this isn't an end-all-be-all list).

Also, don't pick the first co-packing kitchen you tour. There could be better kitchens that suit your company's needs. For example, I should have looked further before choosing my first co-packer. She ended up far too large for us. That mistake cost us several thousand dollars.

Don't make the same mistake I did.

I've seen many food businesses crash and burn because of strained co-packer relationships. Their product isn't the same, quality drops, and you not only have an upset producer, you have a frustrated co-packer -- not a good mix, my friend, not a good mix.

Credibility of your co-packer is more important than price.

You're *marrying* your co-packer. The only difference? There's no ring. But there's months of planning, people to talk to, and of course you want the event to go off without a hitch.

How do I know my co-packer is credible?

Credibility is something you want in your bank, your contractor, your life insurance provider, and your accountant. But, you also want your co-packer to be credible. It's not just a one-off relationship. You are likely going to be talking to your co-packer several times a week making sure everything is on-track.

The last thing you want is for something to go wrong.

For example, your recipes get leaked, too much of an ingredient goes in the kettle, or you're over-charged on your last invoice.

5 Ways to Know Your Co-Packer is the Real Deal

1. They ask for your scheduled process documents
Your scheduled process documents are like a certificate of occupancy for your home. It lets you live there (or gives you access to the co-packer's kitchen). Without them, the co-packer won't know *how* to produce your product. Sure, you have a recipe, but what about the process? Good co-packers make sure you have a scheduled process. That way your product comes out the same way every time.

2. They sign a Nondisclosure agreement
Button up your legal documents before you agree to any co-packing. And one of the most important is a NDA - or a nondisclosure agreement. What this does is protects you and your co-packer from leaking or sharing your recipe. Because we all know if Grandma's blueberry jam recipe gets out, it's all over. Protect yourself. And the true sign of a great co-packer is someone who covers the legal bases first - before you step foot in the door.

3. They produce for large companies and brands
It's like social proof for the food industry. Large brands produce with reputable companies. For example, my first co-packer packed

for King Arthur Flour and Purely Elizabeth -- both companies I'd heard of. My second co-packer produced for much smaller brands, but I found the led to more credibility because she was a small producer herself. But, be warned - large companies may sound cool, but the kitchen might not be the best fit for your company.

4. They are upfront about costs and additional fees
All I can think of is a used car salesman who sells you the car for a flat-fee and then tacks on hidden fees and charges. You don't want to buy a car from him! And you definitely do not want to work with a co-packer who willy-nilly throws line items on your invoice. You need to know the costs up-front and if there are any other potential fees you *could* incur while producing at the kitchen.

5. They view you as a partner - not just a blank check
Co-packers need to make money. But, they should be your friend, too. A lot of people are in business for the money (which ironically may never come in the copious amounts they hope it does). But, genuine, credible co-packers are there to help you through the tough times, solve your food production problems, and be your business partner. Sure, it helps that you pay on time, but keep this in mind as you search for a co-packer. You want a partner.

With credibility in check, it's time to find out what these co-packing facilities are all about. You can find information on their websites and by touring the facility. Let's explore how to get in touch with your potential co-packers and learn more about them.

Narrow your list down to 1 - 3 possible co-packers.

If you're lucky, you've got variety - list of co-packers to choose from. If you do, narrow them down to 1-3 and go through this co-packer evaluation process below. You won't be wasting your time and you'll ask all the right questions:

1. Do a phone interview first
Don't get in your car, drive an hour, and meet with your chosen co-packers quite yet. They could be the wrong fit. You wouldn't want to waste all that money and time would you? That's why I recommend starting with a phone interview. That way, you're comfortable, at

your desk, and have your list of questions in-front of you. Oh, and speaking of questions…

2. Ask the hard questions
This is your food product we're talking about. You don't want to have any surprises when it comes to figuring out who to choose to produce it. That would be a lot of regret, wouldn't it. You want to make sure you make the right selection. Ask the tough questions:

How do you process a product recall?
You don't want any joking around or laziness when it comes to product recalls. Make sure they have a process in place that they follow and product can be recalled within an hour. Many kitchens with third-party certifications are usually quick because they have systems (and software) in place to help you with a recall. It's likely it won't happen, but you want to be sure there's a process in place if it does.

Have you had any productions errors occur and what did you do to correct them?
This is a big one for me because of personal experiences, but it could happen to you to. Ask them if they've screwed up. This tells you if they're honest and handle situations well while under pressure. It's fine if they're able to refocus from the error, but did they communicate with the client when it happened or did they wait until production was completed?

Will I be notified of price increases before being invoiced?
It all comes down to money. Before you're blindsided by price increases or mysterious line items on your invoice, ask to be notified about price increases as soon as possible. That way, if you need to look for a new co-packer you can. Know what you're being charged for and find out if your co-packer is up-front about it.

Who pays for the third-party inspections?
Remember all of those inspections I talked about earlier? Well, they're expensive. And it's important to outline who pays for the inspection. Is it the co-packer? The producer? Or can it be multiple producers? Find this out earlier rather than later as it may be a

determining factor in your selection. Unplanned inspections are costly to small food companies.

Is there a contract I need to sign?
To get started with many co-packers, you'll need to sign a contract. Make sure the contract contains a non-disclosure agreement (NDA) which protects your co-packer from stealing your secret recipes. The contract may only be put in the table if you're looking for better rates and agree to produce a certain amount. That means, if you agree to produce 100 days of the year, your co-packer will likely give you a price break because their facility is guaranteed to be full because of you. As always, read the contract over a few times to make sure you're not being taken advantage of. Be cautious of up-front fees, additional charges, and what happens with breach of contract.

What other fees are associated with making my product?
Speaking of different fees, there are several - and they're all discussed at length later in the book. Make sure all of these fees are outlines for you before you sign your contract. Often these fees come as a surprise to many manufacturers and it hurts their profit margins. Even if you don't expect to pay them when you start, expect to pay them within your first year of co-packing.

3. Go for a visit - and bring a foodie friend.
Just like searching for a college, you toured campus, spoke with representatives, and asked questions about campus life. Touring a co-packing facility is the same experience. Except, this time, you don't want to bring your parents along. Instead, bring another food producer or someone who knows the ins and outs of the industry.

Why would you bring along someone?

Generally, food entrepreneurs have this sense about each other. They know who to trust and who not to trust.

If you know a food entrepreneur, ask them to come with you. They'll be honest with you and the co-packer. If you won't ask the hard questions, they will. Here's what to look for when you visit your short-list of co-packers.

What to look for when you visit:

1. Everything on pallets
Things strewn all over the floor is not up to code. All ingredients and other materials need to be kept off the floor. The easiest way for co-packers to do this is use a combination of pallets and metal shelves. Kind of like Costco or BJ's.

2. Lot tracking documents
Ask to see that your co-packer uses a lot-tracking system. Whether it's pen and paper or a large enterprise piece of software, see that lot tracking is being completed. While your co-packer doesn't have to show you another manufacturer's documents, just have them show you the print-outs they use. If they don't participate in lot-tracking, you're going to have a tough time recalling product, should that happen.

3. HACCP Plans and Good Manufacturing Practices (GMP's)
I know, this is the boring stuff (well, exciting to some). Make sure your co-packer is HACCP certified (this includes everything from receiving ingredients to shipping finished product out of the facility) and practices good manufacturing practices. They likely do if they maintain any third-party certifications. Ask to see documentation if you don't see clipboards around the kitchen document processes and critical control points. If you're curious what good manufacturing practices are, take a look at this link from the FDA (it's quite wordy).

4. Hairnets/hats and gloves
It sounds so basic. Wouldn't all food processing facilities use hairnets and gloves? You'd think so, but some skip over the easy things that keep your food product safe. I've been in facilities that don't use hairnets and gloves and I've also been in facilities that have all guests wear chef's jackets, hair nets, and gloves. Plus, they have you sanitize your shoes in a footbath as you enter the kitchen (this was a large commercial facility). Keep in mind, all facilities are different and have to abide by different regulations based on the certifications and inspections they have. Regardless a head covering

and gloves are musts -- and this may be included in the GMP's from above.

5. General cleanliness

Again, obvious. But, a clean kitchen means you're witnessing a well-oiled machine. The floors should be clean of debris, the sinks shiny, and the shelves organized. Ask if the kitchen is cleaned and washed down after every production. The last thing you want is remnants from another product in your product, just to push units out the door.

6. Updated equipment

Old stuff breaks. New stuff (hopefully) doesn't. Try to find out when the equipment at your prospective co-packer was brought in and when it may be replaced. Old equipment may break more easily than new equipment. And for that reason, you want updated equipment. Remember you get what you pay for, too.

7. Proper storage

If there's anything I've learned, it's that co-packers never seem to have enough storage. And they charge for it if they're tight on space (see the part about hidden expenses later in the guide). Storage is important because you want to know the co-packer can handle your growth. When you order a couple hundred cases of glass, it needs a place to go. And so do all of your ingredients. Make sure your co-packer has some room to spare (even if you have to pay for it).

8. Good rapport between the kitchen manager and employees

How do employees interact with each other? How do they interact with their manager? The relationship between employee and manager is crucial because you don't want an employee sabotaging your production just because they aren't happy with their boss. Look for open body language, laughing/joking, and employees who respect their manager.

While there's a lot more to look for, these 7 things are the most important. They make a huge difference between which co-packers move to the top of the list and which fall to the bottom.

Now that you've visited a couple co-packers and seen their kitchens, it's time to evaluate the best co-packer for the job. And it goes far beyond what you like and didn't like. Here's a couple things to think about.

Questions to ask yourself after you visit all of your co-packers:

1. Did I get along with the co-packer?
As I've stated earlier, your co-packer is like your significant other. You deal with them almost every day, know their quirks, and their faults. Your co-packer should be just like your best friend. Were they approachable? Did they ask questions about you - not them? Did they introduce you to their employees? I bet you enjoy working with nice people - people with integrity. Evaluate how you felt talking to the kitchen manager. If they weren't the right fit, that's your first red flag -- move on.

2. Were there any warning signs?
What didn't you like about the kitchen? Were there things the kitchen needed to work on? If there were any warning signs, are they able to be worked through with you or the co-packer? You have to be able to start off on the right foot. Otherwise, it won't be a great relationship.

3. Can I grow with this company?
As noted by the need for lots of storage, the co-packers needs to have the ability to grow with you. Otherwise, you'll be looking for a new co-packer in a short period of time. That's something we'll talk about later, too. With any company that gets started, you expect to grow. Find a co-packer who is willing to grow with you.

4. Are they able to produce anything else besides my type of product?
This is thinking ahead a little bit, but does the co-packer have the ability to produce anything else? Just because you make spaghetti sauce, doesn't mean you won't start making seasoning mixes, garlic bread, and pizza sauce. Having a co-packer with a diverse product mix means it's easier for you to expand your product line.

5. Are the costs associated reasonable to produce my product?

When you tour a co-packing facility, you'll likely go over all of the costs associated with co-packing (and there are a lot). What it comes to is can you afford it? You may have stumbled on the best facility in a 200-mile radius, but do you have enough cash in the bank to do a run? As you'll learn later, when I started out, I almost ran my bank account to $0 -- and it was frightening.

Now that we're on the topic money, it's time to get down to numbers. The costs of co-packing can either be straight-forward or complex. I've dealth with both. And the hard part is every co-packer is different.

Let's explore the finances of co-packing below.

How much does it cost to work with a co-packer?

After visiting and talking with several co-packers, it's time to take a hard look at the numbers. You need to know if you're going to make money. After all, why would you co-pack if you're going to lose money, right?
There are three ways co-packers charge. All of them have their pros and cons. While you may be able to work out a deal with your co-packer, generally fees are fees unless you sign an annual or multi-year contract.

While this section is quite numbers heavy with several examples, I'll try my best to make it simple for you. I'm not a big fan of numbers either.

Take a deep breath and dive in!

Three Ways Co-Packers Charge:

The three ways co-packers charge are meant to meet the needs of every manufacturer. Sometimes the rates are determined on a case-by-case basis, but many co-packers keep their fees the same just to maintain their own sanity.

1. Flat Day Rate

This is simple. One flat fee for the entire day. For example, each day you produce costs you $500. This means you need to produce as many units as possible in that 8-hour day to reduce your per-unit labor cost.

2. Per Unit Rate

Also simple. You pay per unit produced. Usually this is somewhere between $0.25-$0.50. Anything higher, and you likely won't make any money.

3. Per Hour Rate

If your production only takes a half day or you need extra help, you may get offered an hourly rate. Rates of $25-$80/hour are typically depending on the equipment you use.

The most common fees are flat day rate and per-unit. It's rare to see a per hour rate unless you're just doing prep for production and there isn't a whole lot to finished goods.

Something to note here:

You could also lock in a contracted rate. If you're new and can't guarantee demand (like many small food producers), you'll likely be stuck with a day rate that won't go any lower.

Co-packers do that because they're unsure of your likelihood to stick around. Most food companies are gone within a few years. However, if you're a large company with consistent production runs, you're more likely to get a contract with lower rates.

While we're on the subject of contracts and lower rates....

Let's talk about the fees you probably didn't come across when talking with co-packers. Just like the house analogy from earlier, if you're buying a house that seems too good to be true, it probably is. There could be hidden damage which would cost you thousands of dollars.

Same with co-packers.

A day rate is just one part of the fees you incur. As co-packers become more in demand, they're looking for every possible way to make money. After all, they don't seem to be in short supply of possible food manufacturers, do they?

Below, you'll find a short list of fees that you could rack up while working with a co-packer. It's important to keep these in mind when you're selecting someone to work with. Often times, these costs aren't associated with manufacturing though. But, your net profit margin takes a hit when you add in the unexpected operating costs.

Here we go....

The Hidden Fees Most Co-Packers Won't Tell You About

1. Receiving fees
Even if you source and ship your ingredients to the co-packer, they may still charge you to receive your product. For example, when I would ship glass jars to my first co-packer, they would charge me $20 to receive it. Turns out, I was charged that amount for anything received by them. From that point on (with the exception of glass), I hand-delivered everything. Look for receiving fees to be around $25 for each delivery.

2. Ingredient prep fees
This one makes sense (to me), but make sure you incorporate it. Ingredient prep is typically charged by the hour. Let's say you use fresh peppers. Well, your co-packer isn't going to give you time for free to prep them, are they? This either leads you to use ingredients that require less prep (or not prep at all) or consider raising your prices to incorporate this added cost. Prep fees typically run $25-$50/hour because the facility not only has to cover labor cost, but they have to make some money, too.

3. Pallet storage fees
Space is a hot commodity in co-packing. And co-packers charge for it, too. Mainly because many food entrepreneurs (probably yourself included) don't have the room to store 50# bags of sugar, a pallet of glass, and thousands of units of finished product. What's it typically cost? Be prepared to pay between $25 and $100/month per pallet.

The rate goes up when you're looking for refrigerated or frozen storage.

4. Consulting time
Unfortunately, you can't pick your co-packer's brain forever (I know, wouldn't that be great?) That means your next invoice might have a line item for consulting on it. Whether you talked about pH, HACCP, or distribution strategy, consulting is a good chunk of change. Fees range from $50-$250/hour for food consultants.

5. Third-Party Fees
Third-party audits, required for shelf-space at many major grocery chains, cost a ton of money - upwards of $2,000. If you're the only producer looking for the certification, you're likely to be footing the bill. You're lucky if 2 or 3 manufacturers need the certification because you can split it. And the other certifications like gluten-free, non-gmo, and kosher, all cost money, too. Not only is this a cost you should plan for, but watch for it on invoices from your co-packer as well.

6. Order Fulfillment Fees
Shooting over an email with a purchase order is easy - just hit send. But, for your co-packer it takes time to process your order, get it packed up, and put on the truck. Plus, it takes them away from other activities (like making more product). If you're co-packer offers order fulfilment, be prepared to pay a flat rate plus a per-case rate of $0.25-$0.50.

7. Ingredient Sourcing Fees
There are co-packers out there who will help you through the entire production process, including ordering all of your ingredients. Yes, they do exist. Ordering all of your ingredients is tedious and can take hours if you have a lot of products. Outsourcing this to your co-packer is an option. There's likely going to be a delivery rate (see above) and a percent markup 10-20%. The big question is, are you willing to have 10-20% increase in your raw materials cost for someone else to pick up the phone or order online? It's a fee I personally opted out of, but other companies are willing to pony up the big bucks.

8. Clean-up Fees

Does your product make the kitchen look like a disaster zone? Then you might need to pay clean-up fees to get the kitchen back to normal before the next production. I haven't seen it happen with co-packers too much, but this happens a lot with shared commercial kitchens.

9. Casing Your Product

For many food companies who order bottles and jars (many of you) to package their product, it's often the case where a case box doesn't come with the glass. That means every 12 or every 6 units needs to go in it's own box, labeled, and taped up. That'll cost you, too. $0.50/case usually.

While many of these (with the exception of ingredient prep and ordering fees) are operational costs and not directly related to the manufacturing of your product, they should be taken into consideration.

If you're charged for all of these "hidden" fees, you're likely looking at an additional $300-$500/month in expenses. If you're growing, it's an investment. But, if you're just starting out, look at ways to cut costs and avoid paying these fees.

Now, let's look at some examples:

Here's the background: You make jelly and need to find a co-packer to produce 1,000 units. Let's look at each scenario above, with a mix of fees thrown in.

Flat Day Rate:

- Day rate: $750 for an 8 hour day
- Units produced: 1,000
- Cost per unit: $0.75

That's pretty high for production. But, let's make it a bit more complicated. Let's say you had three shipments received for that production and you had a couple of prep hours the night before:

- Day rate: $750 for an 8 hour day
- Receiving fees: $60
- Ingredient prep: $100
- Units produced: 1,000
- Cost per unit: $0.91

Your labor cost per unit just increased 21.3%

And that's just your labor cost. Nevermind your ingredients, packaging, transportation costs, and other fees. The increase needs to be passed all the down your distribution channel, up to your customer or you'll be making less money.

What are the downsides to paying a flat day rate?

1. Fluctuating per unit rate
Every time you produce, you have no idea how much your labor is going to influence your product cost. One week, your product is cheap to produce. The next? Something goes wrong and your cost spikes. It's tough to control.

2. Pressure to produce as much as you can
When I was just starting out, I was paying a flat day rate. That meant I needed to produce close to 1,000 units just to break even. And I didn't have the demand to meet the supply. When I produced less, my costs went up. It's just part of the numbers game.

3. Tight cash flow
When you pay several hundred dollars a day for use of a co-packing facility and you're doing it weekly, it adds up. Then you've got jars, caps, ingredients, transportation, and time. That's a lot of money. Some production runs have cost me upwards of $2,500. And that was just to get off the ground.

Per unit pricing

This is the pricing model my co-packer currently uses. It allows for greater flexibility, based on demand of your product. That means you can make 10 cases of one product and 5 of another. Let's look into it further.

Per unit price is typically $0.30-$0.80/unit depending on your process.

If you have a lot of manual labor attached to your products (like preparing fresh produce, hand-filling, hand-labeling, etc) your per-unit rate will be higher.

Let's look at an example:

- Units produced: 1,000
- Cost per unit: $0.30
- Prep of ingredients: 2 hours at $30/hour = $60
- Total labor cost: $0.36/unit or $360

See how your labor rate, even with added prep is almost half the cost of a day rate? Now, assuming you're ingredients aren't too expensive, you've got an opportunity to make money here. This means you can go to retailers and distributors and be confident about your pricing structure.

Now, this is not to say that flat-day rate doesn't work. It does. It works for larger companies who are able to produce in volume. If you're just getting started, try to find a co-packer who will produce your product using per-unit pricing.

What are the downsides to per unit pricing?

1. May require production minimums
Your co-packer isn't going to make a case of your product. They're going to require a minimum production yield. Why? Because they need to have a certain volume in the kettle so that it functions properly. For example, a 20-gallon kettle requires at least 3 gallons of ingredients to properly heat and produce product.

2. Prep-time may be an added expense
You can assume that per unit pricing is a baseline cost of doing business. Then, there's likely to be prep time and other fees like I

described above. Yes, this increases your per-unit price, but it's likely to still be less than flat day rate.

Per hour rate

While rare, it's also possible that co-packers charge a per hour rate. This is good for companies with fast productions and little cash.

If a shared kitchen is producing your product for you -- or helping you during production -- an hourly rate is likely applied.

Let's look at an example:

- Units produced: 1,000
- Workers used: 2
- Hourly charge: $25/hour
- Hours: 5
- Total labor cost: $0.25/unit or $250

Now, there's one big distinction here: You're in the kitchen, too. Let's add your labor into the mix - so that you have 3 people producing product at $25/hour. (If you value your time at more money, you can increase the number).

- Units produced: 1,000
- Workers used: 3 (including yourself)
- Hourly charge: $25/hour
- Hours: 5
- Total labor cost: $0.375/unit or $375

Just by adding yourself into the labor mix (because you would have to pay a third person if you weren't there), you increased your labor cost by $0.12/unit.

And another question you're probably asking….

Why are you hiring people for $25/hour? The people helping you work for the facility. They know how to use the equipment. They know how to abide by HACCP guidelines. They're worth $25/hour. Your actual charge may be less.

Looking to figure out your co-packing costs? Because you bought the Ultimate Guide to Co-Packing, you get exclusive access to the co-packing calculator. Access it here:

http://www.gredio.com/copacking-calculator

That's the quick summary of co-packing costs. Use the calculator above to help you make an informed decision about which co-packer would work best for your company and what the cost is going to be if you're moving production out of your home or smaller facility.

With cost under your belt, it's time to make a selection. You've talked to many co-packers on the phone. You've toured their facility and nailed down all costs associated.

Don't just pick one.

This is a strategic decision for your company just as much as it's a financial one. Take time to sit down and think about which facility you're going to select and why. It's truly a make or break moment.

Once you've made your decision, there's lots to do. Let's take a look at what's needed to get the ball rolling with your co-packer.

Selecting a co-packer

Woohoo! You did it. You've made it through the lengthy research process, asked the tough questions, and found a co-packer to work with.

Now, it's time to get ready for day one of production. But before then, there's a couple things you have to cross off your to-do list first.

How to make sure you have your bases covered:

1. Notify them of your intent to have product co-packed (call them)

Your co-packer probably won't follow up with you, so give them a call. Let them know you've selected them to co-pack your products. Ask them about next steps and get your paperwork in as soon as possible.

2. Get a non-disclosure agreement signed immediately

Speaking of paperwork, one of the first things you should do is get both parties (your company and the co-packer) to sign an NDA. Sign it before you talk about process or send your recipes over. The last thing you want is stolen recipes!

3. Make sure you have your suppliers lined up

Moving to a co-packer likely means buying ingredients and supplies in bulk - rather than just running to the grocery store. Spend time identifying suppliers who sell your products and cost everything out. Sometimes (believe it or not), ingredients are still going to be less expensive from the grocery store than in bulk. I'm told it's a supply and demand issue. (It's why we still buy vinegar from Costco and get weird looks!)

4. Pad your bank account for unforeseen circumstances

When you start a food business you're often told to see how much money you need and double it. The same is true when moving to a co-packer. You never know what could go wrong or if you need extra money for increased production. Make sure there's a couple extra thousand dollars just in case something happens and you didn't plan on it.

With your co-packer lined up, legal out of the way, suppliers located, and money in the bank, you're ready to enter the fun-filled world of co-packing. Don't worry, I'll walk you through step-by-step and give you solutions to problems you might run into.

Starting to work with your co-packer

It's kind of like the first day of school. You need to have all of your paperwork in order, dressed in the right clothes, and make new friends. And not to mention those lists you get of the stuff your kid needs. If you think of your kid as your company and the list preparar as your co-packer, here's the list of things you need.

What your co-packers needs from you:

1. Scheduled process (optional for some, but recommended for all)
If you make an acidified food (like mustard, jam, pickles, salad dressing), you need a scheduled process. A scheduled process is a document that states your production methods are sound. It also states critical control points, like pH and fill temperature. Scheduled processes can be completed at several college campus across the US like Cornell, University of Maine, and NC State.

Scheduled process are needed by your co-packer so they know how to produce your product. Plus, they're going to want to know any "production secrets" you may have like prep of fresh produce, order of operations, etc.

2. Certificate of Insurance
From day one, you should have $1 million in product liability insurance and $2 million in general aggregate. This products you, your products, and your company from a lawsuit (which hopefully never happens). You may also have to name your co-packing facility as additionally insured. This is sometimes included in your annual premium. If not, it's $25-$50 per additionally insured party. This protects your co-packer from liability of your products.

3. Your production dates
How often are you going to need space? How much product will you be producing? Should you schedule these dates ahead of time? Communicate all of this to your co-packer because you need to get penciled (err...pened) in to their calendar. The last thing you want is to not be able to meet demand because you can't get on your co-packer's schedule! That would be killer.

I like to forecast demand (or at least try) 6 months out and schedule productions accordingly. To give you an example of how crazy I am, I have production scheduled for the entire year of 2014 - 3 months ahead of time. It's better to have more production dates than you need and cancel them than not enough.

4. Information about incoming shipments

I like to provide my kitchen manager with a heads up when big shipments are coming in - like hundreds of pounds of mustard powder or pallets of glass. I ask her when a good delivery time would be and order accordingly. This not only helps her to anticipate when large deliveries will be happening, but it's respectful and puts me on good terms.

5. Honest and Open Communication

While this isn't a tangible item, it's incredibly important. Why? Because you could forget to tell your co-packer about a process change or be upset with something and hold a grudge - neither are good. I tell my co-packer pretty much everything if it relates to our working relationship. She helps me solve problems and I help her solve problems. The relationship was built on honest and open communication -- and it should always stay that way.

With all of your paperwork in, you're ready to get your first production run at your new facility under your belt. But, don't just let it happen. Be proactive and show up at your production. See how everything works and where there could be improvements.

Before you walk in that door, here are a couple things to think about before, during, and after after you fire up the kettle.

How to make your first co-packing experience a success

Note: You may be using your first production to test and scale up your recipe. This is a critical step if you don't have scaled recipes. From weighing out your ingredients to making sure your spice blends are right when you increase production, **do not skip this step.** Sure, it might cost you money, but it's better to screw up a 5-gallon batch of product than 200, right? Glad we agree there.

Produce what you need:

Similar to above, produce what you need, even if this means an increased per unit cost. Producing excess product puts you in a bind because then you have to sell that product. And if you don't have retailers, distributors, or customers lined up to take the product off your hands, it'll sit there and go past code. Produce to demand. If you need to increase by 10-20%, that would be fine, too. That way, you have a little extra in case you get a spike in demand.

Stay calm and collected:
Your first production can quickly put you in a state of frantic hair-pulling. Take a deep breath. Your co-packers have years of experience under their belts. You're in good hands. Of course, that doesn't mean problems aren't going to happen. On my first production day, I brought in the wrong salt (yeah….). I panicked because I needed a significant amount. Luckily salt is cheap and my co-packer has extra on hand. Learn from me. Everything will be ok. You'll get help and figure it out.

Don't critique:
Your co-packer is going to do things differently -- simply by nature of who they are and the equipment they're using. Let them work through your recipe. What you do on your stovetop at home is going to be significantly different to how you make your product in bulk. And you never know, your recipe may end up better in the end because of it. Several of my mustards have better consistency and texture after being made in bulk. All thanks to ideas my kitchen manager had. Watch and learn. Don't critique until you're finished.

Debrief at the end:
When you've cleaned the kitchen up, talk with your production manager and kitchen manager to review what went right and wrong. Bring up the success of the days and areas you think need to be improved -- either on your end or the co-packers end. This opens the door with honest communication. While some of it may be tough love, when you drive home you'll be glad you got everything you wanted off your chest.

Your first production is likely to be smaller. This is the time you should work the kinks out. Get ingredients down, production process down, and picking up of finished goods sorted out.

But keep going to your first few productions. Yes, I realize you are paying a co-packer to make your product, so you shouldn't have to be there. But, this is the quality of your product we're talking about. Hear me out:

Here's why you need to go to your co-packing facility for your first three production runs:

Oversee the transition from kitchen to co-packing
If you have several product lines, chances are everything won't be made on the first day. When you're producing a product that's new to the co-packer, it's important to be there if something goes wrong. I've sent several new recipes to my co-packer, scaled up and ready to go, only to find out they were production nightmares. Be there.

Make sure your kitchen manager is producing your product correctly
Wouldn't it be a bummer if you showed up and your product wasn't what you expected it to be? It's happened to me twice. And I'm going to tell you both stories.

Story #1
I wanted to make small jars of mustard. I ordered 4 oz jars that would fit a little bit less mustard in them, so our net wt was actually around 3 oz. My labels said net wt. 3 oz. My jars were filled to 3 oz. And it left a huge gap between the product and the cap. Not only did it create an inefficiency in our process, but I wasn't told about the problem until I came to pick up the product.

What should have been done? I should have received a phone call from my co-packer explaining the problem. The jars could have been filled to the top and labels reprinted. Instead, I awkwardly sold what looked like empty jars of mustard.

Story #2
Oh, our horseradish mustard. It was the best seller (up until we started selling Maple Wholegrain). And then it all changed. I went down to pick up finished product. I was met with this "We accidentally double the horseradish, but we think it tastes better anyway." Ok. Panic set in. My costs just increased on the product about 10%. Plus, this was the way I had to make it moving forward. But, I didn't know about the problem until I had 100 cases of it in

the back of my SUV. While it ended up being a good problem to have (people liked the mustard with more horseradish), it still was cause for concern about what else could happen.

What should have been done? Better communication. The recipe should have been scrapped and started over with product made to our specifications. Instead, my co-packer ran with it.

While I certainly hope everything goes smoothly with your co-packing experience, know that it might not. Know that you may have to make decisions on the fly, sprint to the grocery store to remedy the situation, and then go back to complete production. It's happened to every co-packing food producer I've talked to - nothing goes smoothly when you're just starting out.

Once you've completed your first couple of runs, everything should be falling into place (unless you have problems like I did!).

This means you get more time to focus on sales, instead of spending time slaving over a hot oven. But, it's important to keep lines of communication open with your co-packer.

As you build trust, credibility, and a better working relationship, your co-packer starts to become a lot more than a producer of your product. Let's explore this idea further.

How to establish a better relationship with your co-packer

Co-packers are married to your product. They make it for you. They heat up the kettle, preheat the oven, and package it. And some of them even do all of the ordering of your ingredients.
That's an incredible amount of control for your company.
Putting that much trust into a team can be a frightening experience. And a relationship you don't want to jeopardize.
That's why I wanted to share some tips to make sure you keep your co-packer happy:

1. Refer new business

I know you've got at least one goal for your company. I bet it's making money. Am I right? Probably. And the same goes with your co-packer. They're a business, too. So, whenever you're at a farmer's market or chatting up a demo guy at your neighborhood grocery store, keep your co-packer in mind. They'll love you when you refer business their way. Plus, you may even get a discount out of it. Cha-ching!

2. Stay organized

We've all got a million things going on with our food businesses – ordering ingredients, production, shipping online orders, filling purchase orders, trying to land distributors. It's a lot. And you've got to stay organized with everything – especially your co-packer. Make sure you communicate when everything will arrive, the amount you'd like to produce, and other important details. That way there's no surprises on production day.

3. Produce with them

I make sure to hop in on a production at least every quarter. I do this to make sure things are going smoothly and product is being manufactured to my standards. You might catch things you don't want to see, but at least you'll be able to nip them in the bud for the next production.

4. Let them about upcoming products

I always give my co-packer advanced noticed about what we're planning to do next. She typically has a few ideas and gets excited when we launch a new product. For example, when we introduced a holiday mustard in the winter of 2013, I sent over a recipe, but we talked about how the process could be improved. She executed the different process and we ended up with a much better product (and nothing stuck in the filler!).

5. Think about how to make their life easier.

Can you let them know when deliveries are coming. Can you do some of the prep work yourself to save money and prep hours? When you realize all your co-packer does for you, you'll want to return the favor. Be accommodating, send them a holiday card, or make your process easier? They'll appreciate it!

Why work on your relationship? Aren't co-packers just supposed to make your product? Yes, that's their main priority, however, you want to be on their good side. As Rocky DeCarlo from **Rocky's Hot Sauce** says:

"Pay the co packer 50% up front with your order and pay the balance when the product is finished or you pick up your product. Don't be late paying them. Everybody [in any business] likes to get paid ASAP especially when they are laying out there cash for your product. That also gives you some leverage when you need a favor, quick delivery, partial run etc. Nobody likes being a bank for someone else."

You're a food entrepreneur. They're a co-packer. You help each other be successful. Tread lightly when it comes to your relationship with your co-packer. Remember, they make your product. Keep them happy so that they're more likely to bend over backwards for your company when you need it most.

With the relationship sorted out, let's move on.

Next I want to talk about the problems you may encounter with a co-packer and what to do about them.

What if there's a problem with my co-packer?

It's never smooth sailing when you produce a food product. And problems happen with your co-packer, too. Below, you'll find a couple common problems and how to solve them.

5 possible problems you may run into with your co-packer:

1. Your recipe isn't followed correctly
Yep - this does happen from time to time. Mistakes happen. We're all human, right? But, this could cost your business thousands. As you read above, your co-packer may miss-weigh an ingredient and not know it until it's too late. Fortunately for me, it only resulted in a

few pennies of increased cost per unit (and a better product). But, if your recipe isn't followed correctly, let your co-packer know what you'd like done differently. You've done this before. They should be happy to take your suggestions.

2. You run out of ingredients
Either you over-buy or you don't have enough. It's not good either way. Too much of ingredient means your cash is tied up. Not enough? Well, you may not be able to produce to demand. And that ultimately creates frustrated distributors, retailers, and customers. If you've got the flexibility, run out to grab ingredients at the grocery store. Yes, it increases the cost of your product, but it also saves the day. (and a potentially wasted production). Alternatively, you could simply scale back your production to align with the ingredients you have on hand.

3. You have to throw out an entire batch of product
It happens. And it's happened to my company. Unfortunately, I found out after the product was produced. I had 40 cases of bad product. But, it wasn't bad in terms of recalled ingredients. It simply wasn't the right consistency. I don't think the mustard was heated high enough. I was out around $700. I gave the mustard away for free to family and friends. They apparently had no problem with it. But, if you have to toss product because of the lack of an ingredient, you may be able to sell it to a factory seconds store close to you so you can absorb *some* of the cost.

4. My co-packer has no kitchen time available
Sometimes you get a large purchase order and there's no available kitchen time to meet the purchase order deadline. I've been stuck in that situation many times - and it's not fun. Here's what you can do:

- See if your co-packer can switch days with someone else - that's the easiest
- Fill the rest of the PO by producing in your home (if you can)
- Learn from the increased demand and schedule productions ahead of time.

Of course, this also may be a sign you need to look for a new co-packer or kitchen space. Your co-packer may not be able to meet your increased demand. If you want to grow beyond your co-packer's ability, start putting plans in place to move kitchens, or heck, even start your own kitchen.

5. Oops! I need new equipment and my co-packer doesn't want to pay
Well, the first question is how much is it? Could you finance the purchase yourself? If you can't, look at using Kickstarter to get your loyal fans to help you out, apply for a bank loan, or throw your purchase on a credit card (not recommended, but it's an option).

After the cost, ask yourself another question: do you need the equipment? Will it help you produce faster or increase the quality of your product? If you answered yes to either or both of those questions, then purchase the equipment if you can. If not, wait until you can comfortably finance it with profits from the business.

Problems happen. Just like your relationship with your significant other, you work things out. This means honest and open communication is important. Let your co-packer know you've encountered a problem and it needs to be addressed. If they're resistant to your change in process or disagreements escalate, it may be worth looking for another co-packer.

Making the Switch to a New Co-Packer

Have you been having trouble with your current co-packer? Do you keep running into problems you wish would just never happen again?

Then maybe it's time you start the search for a new co-packer. Here's my personal story on why I switched co-packers. It comes down to three main reasons:

1. Cost
It was too expensive. My cost of goods sold was upwards of 70%. That meant no room for operating expenses like marketing and running my online store. This was mainly due to the fact we hadn't quite figured out ingredient costs and we over-ordered everything. Plus, we were charged a flat day rate, driving our per unit cost

through the roof. Not to mention the co-packer was an hour away. That's a lot of time and money I was wasting.

2. Size of Business
My first co-packer was simply too big for my business. I was fresh out of college, some money in the bank, and a successful energy bar company. Now, I wanted to get my mustard company off the ground. The $10,000 I had in my bank account was gone in a matter of months. Why?

Well, to make everything cost-effective, we had to produce 1,000-1,200 units a day. Often times, production spilled over into the next day, too. Every production run cost me several thousand dollars. This taught me I needed to find a smaller operation that produced closer to demand for my product. Somewhere I could produce a couple hundred units to sell at farmer's markets and a few area retailers.

3. Relationship
I just don't think we got along the way I would have liked to. I felt my interests weren't addressed and my first co-packer was focused on larger clients. Clients who co-packed thousands of units several days a week. We were small potatoes. Plus, the error that was made with the horseradish powder (see above) didn't sit right with me. I wasn't consulted when something went wrong several times. And losing trust with your co-packer is a position you never want to be in.

Your reasons to switch co-packers may be different than mine. You may have simply outgrown your co-packer's kitchen or moved your entire operation to the west coast. Whatever the reason, if you're thinking about switching to a new-co-packer, make the process as smooth as possible.

How to make a smooth transition to your new co-packer

1. Tie up loose ends with your current co-packer
You may be in a contract with your co-packer. This would prevent you from leaving, unless there's a stipulation in the contract to cut ties earlier. Regardless, schedule your final production with your co-

packer. Make arrangements to get ingredients and anything else in storage out and to the new location. This may mean storing things in your house or a storage locker in between productions.

It's important to note - leave cordially and on good terms. Explain to your co-packer why you're leaving and that you wish them well. It's likely there aren't many co-packers to choose from in your area. Don't burn bridges!

2. Have recipes (with process) read for your new co-packer
When you move to a new co-packer, get a non-disclosure agreement signed and then send your recipes over. But, don't throw them into unknown territory. Include your scheduled process, ingredient list, and how to make the product. Does it sit overnight? Is it heated to a certain temperature? Do you want your labels put on a certain way? Your new co-packer won't know anything of this if you haven't told them.

3. New kitchen. New process.
From ingredient storage to selecting kitchen dates, and shipping purchase orders, it could all be different from your old co-packer. Be patient as you figure everything out. Your new kitchen manager should orient you to the new space, but there's still going to be a few lessons learned a couple months in. If you're accommodating and relaxed, your co-packer will be, too. And that means they'll produce high-quality product for you.

You don't have to pull your hair out just to switch co-packers. It can be a quick and easy process if you follow these tips. Plus, the switch should make things easier on your cash-flow (unless you're upgrading). And when you're in better shape financially you can focus on growing your business. Did someone say regional brand?

Switching co-packers doesn't come without its bumps along the way. Stay patient as you work with your new kitchen manager to make the transition.

So, what's next?

What's your company look like after you've settled in with your new co-packer? Hopefully it's a lot more stress free and you're able to relax just a bit.

With that, this guide is coming to an end. Thanks for reading all the way down to the end. I really appreciate it.

Now, you're armed with all you need to know about working with co-packers. It's a tough decision to make. I hope you've learned a few things about co-packers. This is what I want you to remember as you navigate the crazy world of co-packing:

1. Find a co-packer who cares.
Someone who has as much passion as you do for your product. Who wants to follow your standard of production. And who you could call a friend.

Why do I want you to put some much time and energy into this decision?

It's not just about money. It's about your company. Your brand reputation is on the line. The second your quality standards plummet, your products aren't purchased. When your products aren't purchased, you go out of business. And that's not how you want to end your company's story, is it?

2. Have a growth mindset.
Companies who co-pack are setting themselves up for growth. Now, because you don't make your product, you can focus on sales, grow your company, and take your business to the next level.

3. Prepare for as much as possible up-front.
Things will go wrong. You will have production nightmares. You will be tight on money (After all, cash is king). And you may disagree with your co-packer. Prepare for as much as this as possible. Panicking when things go wrong won't help you. If you have an action plan to put in place when things don't go your way, you'll be much better off.

4. Know your co-packer is there to help you

They want to see you succeed. They want you to produce more product because it means you're going to spend more money with them. They'll help you plan your recipes, scale up, and produce product both of you are proud to put on grocery store shelves.

With that, let's summarize what you've learned along the way.

Here's the 10-step action plan to finding and working with your co-packer:

1. Determine if/why you need a co-packer
2. Start your co-packer search
3. Calculate costs associated with various co-packers
4. Visit several co-packers to find the right one
5. Get your recipes ready to be co-packed
6. Do a test run with your co-packer
7. Do a big production
8. Strengthen your relationship with your co-packer
9. Continue to evaluate if your co-packer is the right fit
10. Have fun and go build your company

Pay special attention to the last one: *have fun* and go build your company. Co-packing is a business decision to honestly, make your life *easier*. It's a decision that's supposed to help you build your dream.

Jason Luedtke of **Zoroco Packaging** in Caldwell, Idaho, left a comment on a LinkedIn discussion about building a better relationship with your co-packer and had the following to say:

"As a gluten-free/allergen free dry good co-packer I've found that our industry is often thought of as a "necessary evil" instead of an important tool and beneficial partner. Many of our clients have come to us in a very defensive posture and with stories of dissatisfaction.

Our company is dedicated to breaking this mindset and does much in the way of transparency, communication, and customer service to try and earn the trust and loyalty of our clients.

Any solid co-packer should believe in and strive to assist the growth of their clients, it is in our best interest to have our clients grow and expand. The more we can do to see that success the better for everyone!"

Jason's right. Co-packers are partners. As I said earlier in the guide, you're practically married to your co-packer. They are such an integral part to your company (they manufacture your product!) that you need to work with them to help you - and help them.

Where does that leave you?

Use this guide. Read through it once or twice. Take advantage of the resources at the end of the guide - the frequently asked questions, the co-packer list, and the freebies included in the pack.

I hope you got value from this guide. If you have any questions, feel free to reach out to me directly. Here's my contact information:

Michael Adams
Founder of Gredio
michael@gredio.com

About Michael Adams

At just 25 years old, Michael Adams has been involved with three food businesses, each with their own lessons along the way. Here's a little bit about each company:

Adams' Cookie House
When Michael was 15 years old, he couldn't land a job. Eager to pay his own way to movies and hanging out with his friends, he started a cookie business out of his parent's home in Richmond, VT. Taking inspiration from Betty Crocker herself, Michael baked cookies on Friday night and sold them the next morning in-front of the hair salon downtown. Surprisingly, he made a couple hundred bucks a week for a few summers. And this is what got him started in the food business.

Eddie's Energy Bars

Fast forward to senior year of high school. Michael was enrolled in a business class with a passionate entrepreneurial-driven teacher who noticed Michael's potential. Eager to learn more beyond the lessons learned by watching episodes of *The Apprentice* with Donald Trump, Michael worked directly with his teacher to learn the ropes of business. What came from working together was Eddie's Energy Bars.

Michael and his siblings competitively swam for several years. To power through their next race, they'd snack on mass-made energy bars. One day after a race, Michael bit into a chocolate Powerbar. And that was the last Powerbar he ate. He was finished with eating chocolate-flavored duct-tape. He wanted to created his own bar.

Partnering with his Dad, Ed, of which the company was named after, they got to work deconstructing an oatmeal cookie recipe. They took out all the "bad stuff" and replaced it with good whole ingredients like apricots, yogurt, and applesauce. Two years later, they landed on the ultimate cinnamon raisin energy bar.

With a recipe in hand, Michael started to promote the bars at school events and they took off! He asked his business teacher for help writing a press release. They wrote one together in the hour before school started and sent it off to local media.

With a stint on Made-in-Vermont, a local TV series, Michael's small company was off to the races. He garnered press in Backpacker Magazine, Health.com, and even was listed as one of Entrepreneur Magazine's Hot 100 companies in 2009.

He created all kinds of flavors. He had loyal fans, and a growing list of local retailers. Ultimately, the fresh product and lack of fast enough inventory turns, as well as taking up his parent's weekends baking energy bars, was enough for Michael to transition out of the energy biz. But, he had to pounce on his next new idea.

Green Mountain Mustard
While the energy bars and mustard company did overlap for a few months, Green Mountain Mustard prevailed. Launched in May 2010, Green Mountain Mustard set out to be Vermont's Local Mustard.

Using local eggs, butter, and maple syrup, he launched GMM with three flavors -- Sweet Hot, Horseradish, and Jalapeno.

After heading to the local farmer's market and selling out week after week, Michael kept creating new flavors, while making loyal fans at the same time.

Three and a half years later, Green Mountain Mustard is now known for different mustard. For celebrating mustard that isn't bright yellow. Mustard that can be served on more than a ballpark frank.

Michael currently runs this company with his parents, Jeanne and Ed, out of Richmond, VT. You can find Green Mountain Mustard in over 50 retailers across New England and at fairs and festivals throughout the northeast.

Learn more about Green Mountain Mustard at BuyMustard.com

View More Resources at Gredio.com

Gredio.com is one of the best resources for starting and growing your food business.

There's always new blog content, other guides, and video courses for you to explore.

Check it out at Gredio.com

10 Frequently Asked Co-Packing Questions

1. Does co-packing hurt your company reputation?

I don't think it does. On one hand, it's a business decision. It frees you up to grow. On the other hand, customers may want to meet the people who actually *make* the product. They want to make that personal connection. However, your company will get to a point when you need to give up producing your product. Customers should understand that -- as long as your quality stays the same.

2. What if I can't find a co-packer?

There are some parts of the nation where co-packers simply don't exist. That's why many food companies choose to get their products produced several states away. Some NYC companies produce in Vermont. Companies in Florida produce in upstate New York. If you choose to produce out of state, pay careful attention to the shipping charges you'll incur to get a pallet of product back to your warehouse. It may end up being far too expensive. In that case, look for a shared kitchen or consider financing a kitchen with a few other food producers.

3. How do you negotiate a better rate with your co-packer?

You have to have the guaranteed volume to be able to secure an annual contract with your co-packer. Many smaller co-packers will take you on a case-by-case basis because they don't know if and when you may go out of business. With larger, established brands, it's easier to know if they'll go out of business or not.

However, you may be able to negotiate a better per unit rate on some flavors if they require less labor or you're producing more of just that one flavor. I always say, nothing ventured, nothing gained. It's worth asking your co-packer to see if they'll work with you. Often times, they won't want to lose your business.

4. How do I know if a company co-packs its products?

Look on the label. It will either say "manufactured for" or "Distributed by" -- these are typically giveaways that the company doesn't make its own products. You could also just ask, too. A lot more companies are starting to co-pack their products because they need to focus on growing the company.

5. What other service should I look for besides manufacturing?
Full-service co-packers are amazing. Why? Well, because they do everything. But, you'll pay for it. Look for co-packers who provide consulting, nutrition facts labels, UPCs, and ingredient sourcing (they often know of ingredient sources you've never heard of). This way, you'll be able to get more done at one company and have to split services up.

6. What do you do if co-packing doesn't work out?
You can always go back to producing your own products. You're the best at it anyway, right? Or, you can always meet in the middle and start using shared kitchen. Remember, though, you won't be able to have the same flexibility as you had with a co-packer. For many larger companies, it ultimately becomes less expensive to produce products by yourself, using your own production facility.

7. Is there any software to manage everything with my co-packer?
A lot of food producers use pads of paper or Microsoft Excel to help run their business. That can only take so far. I launched Gredio in March 2013 to help food producers handle some of the numbers of their business Unfortunately, I shut the software down in 2014. You can view the blog at Gredio.com.

8. Do co-packers help me transition out of my home kitchen?
When you make the transition from your house to another kitchen, there can be a lot of new things. Whether it's ingredient sources, scaling up, or connections to other producers and retailers, co-packers will help you to a point -- especially with scaling up your recipes. While you'll pay for it, the help is worth it. You co-packers know what they're doing. They know how to grow food companies; because it's likely they've done it before. Don't be afraid to ask for help - and do it early, too.

9. Is there a reason not to leave your home kitchen?
Of course there are. Your house is well-known to you, it's free rent (to an extent), and you have a less expensive state license. But, there comes a time when your home oven only takes you so far. You might need to move to a facility. However, it can be a costly move.

Your supplies increase, your labor increases -- everything goes up. So, you have to think about where you want your company to be. Do you want to stay small and in your home or do you want to take your company to the next level?

10. Are there any industry experts to help you co-pack?
Yes - there are tons of consultants out there - a simple google search reveals a couple of experts, depending on what you're looking for. From process controls, to consultants who help you find a co-packer, they're out there. But, you'll pay for it. Many consultants charge anywhere between $50-$200/hour. Sometimes, however, the consulting expenses could save you thousands of dollars down the road.

Made in the USA
San Bernardino, CA
26 November 2017